THE ORGANIZED HEART

A Woman's Guide to Conquering Chaos

Staci Eastin
Cruciform Press | Released March, 2011

For Todd, who knows my faults and loves me
anyway. And for Adam, Elise, and Jacob. May you
always rest in the grace of our perfect Savior.

– Staci Eastin

D1113948

CruciformPress

"Staci Eastin packs a punch with this short book. But it's a gracious punch, full of insights about our disorganized hearts and lives, which is immediately followed by the balm of gospel-shaped hopes. *The Organized Heart* is ideally crafted for use with accountability partners and small groups. Because of the Holy Spirit's active presence, there is always hope for change. Open this book with that great truth in mind and you'll find much to ponder!"

> **Carolyn McCulley**, fellow procrastinator, is a blogger, filmmaker, and the author of *Radical Womanhood* and *Did I Kiss Marriage Goodbye?*

"Unless we understand the spiritual dimension of productivity, all our techniques will ultimately backfire. In this book, Staci Eastin has provided that all-important spiritual perspective. Instead of adding new rules, she explains how to keep leisure, busyness, perfectionism, and possessions from becoming idols. Encouraging and uplifting rather than guilt-driven, this inside-out approach can help women who want to be more organized but know that adding another method is not enough."

> **Matt Perman**, Director of Strategy at Desiring God, blogger at whatsbestnext.com, and author of the forthcoming book, *What's Best Next: How the Gospel Transforms the Way You Get Things Done*

"Organizing a home can be an insurmountable challenge for a woman. *The Organized Heart* makes a unique connection between idols of the heart and the ability to run a well-managed home. This is not a how-to; instead, Eastin looks at sin as the root problem of disorganization, and strives to help the reader understand biblically how to overcome this problem. She offers a fresh new approach and one I recommend, especially to those of us who have tried all the other self-help models and failed."

> **Aileen Challies**, Mom of three, and wife of blogger, author, and pastor Tim Challies

Table of Contents

Chapters

Print ISBN: 978-1-936760-11-4
ePub ISBN: 978-1-936760-13-8
Mobipocket ISBN: 978-1-936760-12-1

CruciformPress.com
email: info@CruciformPress.com
Twitter: @CruciformPress

One
OUR STORY

Just two days before Christmas, and I was terribly behind. We expected to leave town in thirty minutes and I had just started packing. Todd, my husband, went to get gas, hoping that by dividing the chores we could still get away on time. Meanwhile, I frantically dug through baskets of clean laundry, hoping to find enough matching pairs of socks to see my preschool-age son through the week. Each glance at the clock revealed that I would not finish in time.

I began a mental list of all the reasons I wasn't ready. I don't remember now what they were, but I'm sure I drew from the stock of excuses I always used: unexpected events, needy children, unreasonable demands from others. But as Todd returned, conviction washed over me. None of my excuses were lies, but I wasn't being completely honest. Because while my week had brought a few surprises, I had still managed to find time for plenty of other things—less important things.

When Todd returned home and walked into our bedroom, I looked him in the eye and told him the truth. I was running late because I hadn't prepared. It was all my fault.

I must have eventually finished packing, because we did make it to our parents' homes for Christmas that year. And Todd, who has always been incredibly patient with my slapdash housekeeping, spent the rest of his vacation cheerfully helping me return the house to order.

I wish I could say that my story of holiday chaos was just that—a season, and an unrepeated one—but I can't. One year later I was running errands and half-listening to a Christian radio program about New Year's Resolutions. Listeners called in and listed the changes they wanted to make in the coming year: lose weight, quit smoking, spend more time with their families. At each stoplight I glanced at my to-do list, checking off anything recently accomplished, but also adding new tasks as they occurred to me. As the uncompleted items piled up faster than the completed ones, I once again felt the pressure of too much to do and too little time to do it in. Suddenly I heard the host ask the radio audience to think of our own resolutions, and I tearfully whispered, "I want to be more organized."

You may think I was being too hard on myself. Christmas is a busy time, and it's only normal to feel stressed and rushed then. But that season simply placed a spotlight on a constant reality. My problem with disorganization seemed more apparent during Christmas, but the problem was always there. In fact, my entire adult life could be described as a series of unfinished good intentions: notes and cards never sent (or even bought), dinner parties never thrown, kind words never spoken, calls never made, help never given.

So I come to you as someone who must fight to stay organized every day of her life.

In Pursuit of an Organized Home

My mother and my grandmothers were industrious women who showed me that organization is possible. They managed to keep clean houses, work, volunteer, and still have ample time for family, rest, and leisure. In an effort to be more like them, I have read countless books on home organization, and I own more planners than any person could ever need. I've tried lists, notebooks, note cards, and filing systems; I've posted schedules and spreadsheets; I've bought drawer organizers and closet systems. While all these things helped for a time, none brought the lasting change that I sought.

The systems, after all, require implementation, but my disorganized heart can corrupt a perfect rule and refuse a generous teacher. I can shove unfolded T-shirts into beautiful closet shelves or justify fudging on a sensible daily schedule. But the systems I tried don't get to the heart of why I do that. Most of these books and tools assume that disorganization stems from lack of skill. If I would just follow a certain system, I could enjoy a life of organized bliss. I could float through my spotless house, sail to all my appointments on time, and never feel stressed or rushed again.

Other books blamed my disorganization on childhood traumas or family dysfunctions. Surely my parents had loved me too little (or too much), had praised me too little (or too much), or had disciplined me too little (or too much). If none of those things applied, perhaps I had a chemical or hormonal imbalance. Regardless of the cause, it certainly wasn't my fault.

Other books tried to tell me how lucky I was to have a house to clean. Housekeeping could be such fun; I just didn't know it yet.

I've come to see my disorganization as not due to a lack of skill or knowledge. I know how to keep a home, as I watched that done well all through my growing-up years. And since I already lacked the self-discipline to organize the tasks I knew needed doing anyway, the additional task of filling out a chart or planner just became one more thing to distract me from my priorities. Failing the system seemed inevitable.

Pop psychology didn't help either. Blessed with a happy childhood and loving parents, I can't blame anyone else for my failures: I know my parents taught me better. Nor could I blame any physical problem, for I am in the best of health, and I've always managed to find lots of time, energy, and ability to complete tasks I want to complete.

As for housekeeping being fun? Some of my friends like to vacuum and others enjoy ironing. I have one friend who thinks cleaning out a closet is a fun way to spend a free afternoon (I worry about her). I've always taken great satisfaction in dusting — as long as I don't have to clear clutter beforehand. Pleasure in housekeeping seems subjective, then. It is a necessary task, and some enjoy some pieces of it but simply do the rest. Just as we have different abilities and talents, we will always find some tasks more interesting than others. Why cleaning the toilets must be *fun* is beyond me, but they still must be cleaned, and organizing my days so that such tasks can be accomplished is important.

So the real question is *why* I don't organize my days to do what I believe is important and what I do, in fact, have the skills and training to do. The answer is that I have a motivation problem. I *do* what I do not want to do — and I do *not* do what I want to do.

In Pursuit of an Organized Heart

Naturally organized people gain satisfaction from getting their work done quickly without procrastinating. They have learned to budget their time so that they don't take on more commitments than they can handle. They can easily whittle down their possessions to fit the amount of storage in their homes. When unexpected things come up, they prioritize between the urgent and non-urgent.

And then there is the rest of us. We know we shouldn't put required tasks off until the last minute, but something more pressing (or more fun) always seems to come up first. We know we shouldn't take on yet another commitment, but everything seems so important, and we don't want to let anyone down. Our closets, drawers, and garages overflow with extra stuff, but when we try to clean out, we can't part with any pieces. Some of us may even have spotless homes, but we're exhausted. We feel like we work all the time without any free time to relax and enjoy life the way other people do.

Secular psychologists tell us that we do these things because in our minds the payoff for disorganization is greater than the benefit of organization. We procrastinate because we don't want to do what needs to be done now. We overcommit because saying *No* hurts. We gain excess possessions because we prefer the certainty of having too much to the possibility of not having enough. We seek perfection because contentment feels like compromise. In other words, despite the fact that our lives are spinning out of control, in our twisted minds we believe that living this way is more pleasurable than taking steps to fix the problem.

I think those psychologists are partly right. The disorganization in my life was not due to lack of knowledge or skill and it was not due to a problem in my childhood. Rather, it's a broken belief system: a heart issue, a sin issue. At the end of the day, it's idolatry.

That may sound awfully harsh. You want this book to help you organize your life, not lay more guilt and shame at your feet. Being disorganized may be unhandy, but it's just your personality, right? It's certainly not a sin.

Or is it? Disorganization steals your joy. It causes you to go through your life frazzled and stressed. It causes friction with your husband and makes you snap at your children. It makes you perform ministry tasks grudgingly. It prevents you from developing friendships, because you're always rushing from one task to the next. You don't feel like you're doing anything well, let alone to the glory of God.

The Bible is clear that as Christians, we have tasks appointed to us by God (Ephesians 2:9-10).

We should do everything we do with all our heart because we do it for the Lord (Colossians 3:23). As women, we are instructed to care for our homes and families (Titus 2:3-5). Whether we want to refer to our disorganization as personality quirks or sin, we must fight against anything that interferes with our relationship with God.

We never conquer sin by adding more rules. That's what the Pharisees did, and Jesus chastised them for it. Jesus is interested in more than just outward works; he wants us to perform good works from the overflow of a loving and pure heart. My attempts to get organized always failed because I tried to change my habits without letting the Holy Spirit change my heart. It was only when I saw the sinful motivations behind my bad habits that I could see lasting change in my life.

Starting to Start the Pursuit: Naming the Idols

This book will be different than any other book on organization that you've probably read. I have no schedule to offer you, I won't tell you what day to mop the kitchen floor, and you don't need to buy a timer. Your standards for an organized home and a reasonable schedule will vary with your personality, season of life, and the needs and preferences of your family.

What I hope to do is to help you examine your heart and discover things that may be hindering your walk with God. My goal is not necessarily for you to have a cleaner home or a more manageable schedule—although I certainly hope that is the case. Rather, my hope for this book is that it will help you serve God and your family more effectively, more fruitfully, and with greater peace and joy.

I can't promise that the change will be instant or total. The salvation we receive when we accept Jesus as our savior *is* instant and total, but sanctification—the process of becoming holy, or more like Christ—is a lifelong process. Christ's death on the cross saves us from the penalty of sin, but we still have a sinful nature that we must battle daily. We shouldn't fall under the impression that holiness will automatically come to us while we sit and watch television. Holiness is something we must strive for (Hebrews 12:14), and we must start in the heart. Identifying the heart issues behind your disorganization will enable you to repent of them. Through the strength of the Holy Spirit, you can rid yourself of these idols (Romans 8:13).

It's unfashionable these days to talk about sin, and it's even less fashionable to talk about idolatry. The world likes to tell us that we're beyond that now. When we honestly discuss the sinful attitudes behind our actions, we are often shushed: "You're not that bad! Everyone does those things! You need to have better self esteem!"

But the human heart is the same now as it was in biblical times. We don't have to bow down to a golden statue to worship idols. When we trust in anything other than God for peace and happiness we are essentially practicing idolatry. Only when we see the idols yet in our hearts can we truly "put off the old self" and "put on the new self" (Colossians 3:5-10).

In this book, I have identified four idols that seem to particularly hinder women from serving God effectively. They are leisure, busyness, perfectionism, and possessions. You may find that you only struggle with one or two, or you may discover that your problems have their roots in all four. I will examine all of them so that you, by the grace of God, can identify where your weaknesses lie, and begin to experience a more joyful walk with the Lord.

Explore

1. I'm going to step out on a limb and assume that if you are reading this book, you struggle with staying organized. Which of these areas describe your problem (more than one may apply):

___ Lack of knowledge (not knowing what to do)
___ Lack of skill (not knowing how to do it)
___ Lack of action (just not doing it)

2. In Romans 7:18-20, Paul discusses his desire to do what is right, coupled with his apparent inability to carry that out. What does he say is the cause of this struggle? Where do you see the same struggle in your own life?

3. We tend to think of idols as items or statues that we physically bow before. In Colossians 3:5, what does Paul call idolatry? What's similar between the idols in that list and a physical statue?

Two
PERFECTIONISM

In March 2009, the *St. Louis Post-Dispatch* featured the sale of a 1950s-era home in The Hill neighborhood of St. Louis. From the outside, the frame-style track house appears unexceptional, similar to many other houses found in that part of the city. What made this home so extraordinary was its interior.

The house, which the adult children who grew up there were selling, was in pristine condition, completely unaltered since their parents had purchased it in 1956. Everything from the carpets to the furniture and even the appliances was virtually unused.

Throughout the decades they had lived there, the family spent their time in the basement: they cooked, played, ate their meals, and conducted the rest of daily living surrounded by the basement's concrete floors and exposed ceilings. The boys only went upstairs to sleep in their beds at night and bathe in the bathtub in the winter. The upstairs stove was used

28 times – each year at Thanksgiving. Anytime the family ventured upstairs, they carefully stepped on throw rugs laid out to save the carpet. The furniture was covered in plastic.

The Importance of Excellence

What would you think if you entered such a house? Would you admire the spotless carpet and sparkling kitchen? If you didn't know the price the family paid to keep it that way, would you be tempted to strive for the same standard?

We should aim for excellence in all we do. The goal of perfection has lead to many great achievements in the world of art, athletics, and technology. Physicians, airline pilots, and bridge designers, for example, need to be as close as possible to perfect in their work.

More importantly, Colossians admonishes us to do all our work well, because we're really working for God, not men. That includes all our daily tasks, even those that might not require the same degree of precision as the architect designing a skyscraper. Whether caring for your home and family or working a 9-to-5 job, whatever we do is important and worthy of our best efforts.

Sometimes, though, our goals go beyond striving for excellence. We do not see ourselves as stewards of talents and tasks that God has given us so much as superwomen who must achieve the highest standard or else fail as humans. So the noble goal of working diligently takes a subtle turn. Instead of giving our all and trusting God for the results, we shoot for an impossible goal: perfection.

The Problems with Perfectionism

Perfectionism in its purest form wants the best for God and others. We usually consider it a good thing. In fact, the word "perfectionist" conjures up ideas of someone who does her work well and takes the time to care for important details. But in this chapter, I mean "perfectionism" as that sinful preoccupation with appearances that blinds us to the importance of God's grace and glory.

The other chapters in this book address heart issues that lead to outward chaos: people can quickly spot a messy, cluttered home or an unworkable schedule. But perfectionism is chaos turned inward. The visible life of the perfectionist may seem ideal, but that carefully maintained façade hides a frenzied and wrongly motivated heart.

While excellence is a noble goal, perfectionism as I mean it here is a form of bondage. Instead of making us excited and hopeful, it leaves us irritable and cross. Perfectionists can drown in a sea of details, stressing out over the minutiae of life and missing moments of joy. Perfectionists rarely get the luxury of resting in a job well done, ruminating instead on the minor flaws that spoil their idealistic plans.

Fear of those minor flaws can therefore paralyze perfectionists, making them incapable of any action. If we don't have the time or energy to perform a task to our exacting standards, we may not do it at all. Or if we cannot see that the end result will be just right, we do not even take a first step.

It can be hard to spend time with perfectionists. Friends and family feel pressure to live up to impossible standards, or they feel frustrated by slow action. The perfectionist's wish to control every detail of her environment can strain relationships, often hurting those she loves the most. Thus, we must not take pride in perfectionism, nor provide it as a sanctified excuse for inaction. Rather, we must fight against perfectionism as we aim to become more like Christ.

Perfectionism and Idolatry

If we were honest, we would say that at least sometimes we pursue perfection because we want others — maybe even God — to think well of us and our abilities. In our hearts at those moments, appearances and praise of man are ultimately important, or else we think we must *make* ourselves worthy of God's love. This means that perfectionism has become an idol. Rather than trusting in God to enable us to perform the tasks we must do, we rely on our own power. Instead of finding our joy in following Christ, we scramble to acquire the praise of others. Rather than trusting in God's grace, we foolishly try to earn God's love.

Wanting to do our best for a holy God is a good thing, but aiming for perfection to earn God's favor is not. Perfectionism becomes idolatry when we believe that the quality of our work makes us worthy of God's praise. That is trying to find salvation in what we do, not in what Christ has already done for us.

We should give our all, but we should do so while resting in the knowledge that God esteems us because of Christ's work on the cross, not because of any actions of our own. We bring glory to God when we serve him, but we don't make our salvation more secure when we do something well. The idol of perfectionism therefore competes with the most important desires of our hearts—do we take our ultimate pleasure in who Jesus is and what he has done for us, or do we strive to void his work on the cross because we want to earn our own glory with our own perfection?

Pride in Reputation

Some perfectionists are primarily motivated by how others perceive them. We desperately want to show others our best self and will go to heroic lengths to do so. This goes beyond the desire to maintain a good witness to the world. When we truly want to witness to others, we walk alongside them to show them a better way. We reveal the gospel, which means seeing our great weakness in light of God's sufficient strength. To pretend that our lives can be perfect without the gospel applied deeply and constantly to our hearts is self-righteousness.

It's also unloving, because perfectionism doesn't give: it takes. Instead of working to help others become their best, perfectionists work to gain admiration from others. Instead of pointing others to worship a holy God, we turn the spotlight on our own achievements.

This striving to capture the good opinion of others shows what is really on the throne of our hearts. We cannot serve two masters. When we derive our peace and joy from the praise and admiration of others, it is idolatry. We are not serving God, but our own perceptions of what impresses other people. Our joy and peace do not rest in God and his love, but in receiving the approval of man.

Pride in Talents

God gives all of us gifts with which to serve the church and the world. Some of these are talents that we can develop through natural means, and which we may be tempted to use for our own glory. Consider a musical talent, for example. Music is a gift from God, and it has always had an important place in our worship services. Some people have abundant musical talent, so they can sing or play difficult pieces with little preparation. Others must work harder, practicing for weeks to reach the same level of proficiency.

The ability to do well with little practice should humble you because that great blessing comes only from the hand of a gracious God. Similarly, if you need to practice more, you should rest in the knowledge that God has given you the grace to work diligently and can use your talents mightily. Strive always to do your best, knowing that though you may need to work harder than others, God is sovereign and will use this to make you more like him.

Whether singing a song, cooking a meal, hosting a bridal shower, helping in the nursery, or decorating your home, you can usually find at least someone with more natural talent than you. But if one or more of these things come easily, that is a gift from God, not an indicator of your worth or a tool to secure your salvation. Neither does it mean that God is more pleased with your service if you must work hard.

Romans 14:23 says that anything we do that is

not motivated by faith is sin. Maybe you can sight-read a Beethoven sonata or cook a gourmet meal at a moment's notice. If you do these things with a sincere heart focused on God, he is glorified. In a similar vein, God does not necessarily take more pleasure when we do things that require more effort, especially if our motivations are not sincere.

Pride in Parenting

Many of us struggle with perfectionism in only one area of our lives: our children. Good or bad, our children generally reflect our values and habits, and many of us will stop at nothing to ensure that our children make us look good.

Raising children is a privilege and a serious undertaking, as the Bible often reminds us. The Proverbs admonish us to discipline our children and teach them. The qualifications for church elders set forth in I Timothy and Titus include the ability to manage their children well. We should not underestimate the challenge and importance of parenting our children.

We are often tempted, though, to strive so hard for perfect behavior in our children that we neglect or ignore their heart issues. These may either be the heart issues behind poor behavior, requiring discipline, or a preoccupation with "being good" in hopes of receiving praise, requiring us to help our children better understand their own motivations.

We must remember that only the Holy Spirit can truly change our children's hearts. Just as our salvation came by the grace of God, so will the salvation of our children. Our children are sinners, just like their parents.

While we cannot change our children's hearts, life provides us with many opportunities to minister to and teach our children, thus pointing them to the God who *can* change them. But perfectionists usually miss these chances. We're so busy striving for well-behaved children who make us look good that, in those messy and disappointing and difficult moments, we fail to point our children to the Savior.

A few years ago at a birthday party with my children, another mother pulled me aside and told me that my child had talked back to her. She was embarrassed to tell me, but as my friend, she said that she would want to know if one of her children had behaved the same way.

As she recounted the situation, I began to realize that although my son had been wrong, my friend didn't have the whole story. For one thing, she had given him different instructions from what I had told him a few minutes before. And even though he inappropriately asked "So what?" to get clarity from her, he had only repeated something I said often.

This could have been a wonderful teaching moment. It reminded me how my kids often imitate my behavior. It offered a chance to teach my children the right way and the wrong way to ask questions. It created an opportunity to show them that the words we choose are important, and that they can unintentionally cause offense.

Sadly, I didn't handle the situation with such a gentle or wise approach. Rather than pulling my son aside and explaining what he had done, I publicly scolded him and made him immediately apologize. I didn't teach or explain. I swooped in and acted out of shame, with no interest in the state of my child's heart, but with great interest in the opinion of the other parents. In the end, everyone involved was embarrassed. I worried so much about appearances that I ended up making everybody miserable.

I don't want to imply that my children are never at fault. Many aspects of this incident did require teaching and even admonishment. But in this case, my son had been guilty of mere carelessness — not the blatant disrespect for which I disciplined him. The scene I caused revealed much more about my own heart than his: clinging to my idol of perfect children, I became angry and defensive, not gentle or restorative. The gospel must go deeply into this mother's heart so that I can let go my fear of what others think and parent my children with the gospel as well.

It's All About the Heart

God is more interested in the heart attitudes behind our actions than the actions themselves. We see this in the story of the widow's mite, found in both Luke 21 and Mark 12. Jesus had been in the temple all day, teaching the gospel and watching the people. He had noticed the rich putting their offerings in the offering box, but when a widow came with two small copper coins, Jesus praised her: Her gift was worth more than all the others because she had given all she had.

We usually hear this story taught as a lesson about giving, and rightly so. But because nothing illustrates the motives of our hearts more than what we do with our money, I think it's appropriate to also look at this in the context of our actions and even as we consider the idol of perfectionism.

Jesus spoke some of his harshest words for the scribes and Pharisees because they did everything for the sake of appearance. In fact, in the verses immediately preceding the story of the widow's offering, Jesus says that they will receive great condemnation because they love appearances so much. He says nothing about the quality of the scribes' work, which probably did look impressive to onlookers. But Jesus objected to the pretense behind that work. The scribes got their pleasure from the praise of others, and Jesus condemned them for it.

Then we get to the widow. Out of all the displays

that Jesus had witnessed that day, he highlighted this one as good. The large gifts of gold placed in the offering box throughout the day did not draw his praise, but the meager gift of two copper coins did, and Mark 12:42 tells us that gift added up to a mere penny. The scribes worried most about how their gifts looked to others, but Jesus cares only for the heart motivation behind a gift.

Symptoms of Perfectionism

If your desire for perfection causes you to disregard the heart motivations behind your work or to pursue unreasonable standards, you may be struggling with the same self-righteousness that Jesus saw in the scribes. Like anything else, people struggle with perfectionism in degrees. You may feel the tug of perfectionism in every undertaking, from visible ministry to the state of your sock drawer. Keeping everything "just so" may be such a ruling factor in your life that you constantly feel tired and stressed. Or maybe you are only a perfectionist about one or two things, like your job or your house.

- When company is coming, does your family enjoy the anticipation of opening your home to guests, or do they cringe under your frantic demands to have everything "just so"?
- Are you able to let your children do things for

themselves, knowing that they will learn and grow in the process, or do you continually step in and take over?

- Have you ever decided not to use some gift or talent because you feared comparison with someone else and falling short?
- Have you ever neglected an important behind-the-scenes duty because you wanted to devote more time and energy to a less important but more public one?
- Have you ever been dishonest about the amount of time and effort you put into a project or ministry, claiming that you just "threw something together" at the last minute when you really worked for hours?
- When it becomes apparent that a project will not go as planned, are you more worried about the opinions of others, or the opinion of the Lord?

It can be difficult to determine when we cross the line from striving for excellence to succumbing to a sinful perfectionism. By the time we reach adulthood, most of us have practiced false humility for so many years that we are quite good at appearing humble when we're not. Others of us may feel pious because we work harder at some things than other people do, but this is sinful pride. We may not put ashes on our foreheads and announce that we're fasting (Matthew 6:16-18), but we still hope our toil will bring us extra favor.

The problem with perfectionism lies in the motivation behind it. You should do your best at work and give your employers the job due them, but if you repeatedly let important tasks slide in order to spend time on unnecessary details, your priorities are unbalanced. If the desire for perfection burdens you to the degree that it causes strain in your relationships, or if you find you have trouble relaxing and not worrying, even after all the important responsibilities in your life have been properly seen to, you may struggle with perfectionism.

Finding Rest

Return to the time-capsule house described as this chapter began. The people who worked so hard to maintain it no longer live there. They kept immaculate furniture and carpets but rarely enjoyed them. Perhaps they simply wanted a clean home? Being a good housekeeper is a worthy goal, but if your house is such a shrine that your family cannot relax in it, you need to find a balance in which you and your family can actually live.

I obviously don't know the motivation in the hearts of the parents who owned that time-capsule house. In the article I read, the sons maintained that this kind of behavior wasn't unusual in their neighborhood, which consisted largely of Italian immigrants. Loving family relationships can occur in any sort of physical environment, and tender care in a basement is better than cold neglect in the finest home. Indeed, living conditions in many American basements are still superior to those in many parts of the world.

Nevertheless, I think that house vividly illustrates how the idol of perfectionism is bondage. The sons selling the house said their parents wanted to preserve it for company, but the measures they took to do this prevented their family from living in and enjoying their own home. Maintaining the standard of a perfect home controlled every aspect of their daily lives.

Perfectionism prevents us from living our lives. It prevents us from enjoying our families. It robs us of joy. And most of all, it prevents us from basking in God's grace and serving in the strength that only he can give. God knows our talents, our energy level, and our resources. He alone is perfect, and he can work mightily, so we can trust him.

Explore

1. How can we determine when our efforts have moved beyond striving for excellence to an idolatrous form of perfectionism?

2. Have you ever had something go differently than you planned, only to find that something good resulted from what seemed like a mistake? How might that end result reveal that your original expectations were amiss, or that your original standards were inappropriate?

3. Do you sometimes feel that God finds more pleasure in you when the things He has given you to do go smoothly? How does this square with Scripture, such as John 15:4-5 and Ephesians 6:6?

4. Do you agree that a sinful degree of perfectionism is an attempt to suppress inward chaos? Why or why not? Do your efforts to control things lessen inward chaos or increase it? Think of a specific example from your own life where your attempt to control some situation revealed a lack of faith in God.

Three
BUSYNESS

Women wear busyness as a badge of honor. Commercials show us the fashionable career woman sipping expensive coffee as she dashes off to important meetings in expensive shoes. Families fragment themselves, hustling in and out of minivans and SUVs, eating on the run, shuttling back and forth to sports games and music lessons and school functions.

Those of us in the church have even more to do. Added to the common glut of activities and work are church functions and ministries. We feel the desire and sometimes the pressure to serve, so we stare at our packed calendars and try to cram in one more thing.

We laugh about it with our friends. Comparing schedules can often degrade to a lighthearted game called "Who's busiest?" In our more unguarded moments, we wonder if we can keep it up, but we resign ourselves to the belief that there's no other way.

Women often think they are exercising great faith when they take on too much: "Look what God can enable me to accomplish!" We stay up too late and get up too early, not out of a sense of Proverbs 31 stewardship but because our calendars require us to sacrifice rest. We don't have time to exercise. We throw meals together at the last minute, and the family eats in shifts. When we do have a free evening, family members collapse in exhaustion rather than interact and share.

And what about God? We're often so busy for God that we do not actually serve him in faith. But we simply cannot say no to others' requests or demands: every activity seems so important, and every need seems so great, that we feel we must agree to help.

The result is chaos. Our health suffers and our lives become frantic. We run from one task to the next, and nothing gets the care and attention it deserves. Even if we manage to hold it together on the outside, we feel exhausted and guilty on the inside. In the stolen moments when our bodies are still, our minds are racing – thinking of the next event, the next project, the next day.

So what compels us, when God and family continually get the leftovers of our time and energy, to say yes to the committee, Bible study, or fundraiser? Maybe you have convinced yourself that you like to help people, that you get joy from serving and making people happy. But just because you can do something doesn't mean God has called you to it. When your need to serve controls your daily calendar, you reveal an especially subtle idolatry. This can be rooted in a fear of man or an unbelief in God's ability and timing. Either way, we show that we are not serving in faith, and we are not resting in the grace of God.

What Is Fear of Man?

When a couple in our church had their first baby, a friend of mine called to ask if I would prepare a meal for them. The next day, I planned my grocery list with the upcoming meal in mind. I had recently made a dish that a friend of my teenage son had highly praised, and I decided to make it again. I enjoyed the idea of them enjoying the meal, but my mind suddenly took a detour. Would they enjoy the dish as much as my son's friend had? Would they tell me so later? Would they tell others?

You see how quickly it happens? I want to think my initial intentions were Christlike. I love this couple and wanted to bless them with a meal, but I still have my sinful nature to contend with. My "fear" of what others would think began to steal away those honorable intentions to serve others for the sake of Christ. I wanted praise for myself and cared more about my reputation than the simple joy of doing good. That's fear of man.

What Does Fear of Man Have to Do With My Calendar?

Women who agree to do too much are often driven by the desire to be liked. We commit to things not because we feel the Holy Spirit's urging, but because we want other people to be pleased with us. Or, in a similar vein, we worry that if we don't agree to some request, others will be angry with us or think less of us. We cannot risk disappointment or anger from a friend.

Fear of man indicates that we find our worth in pleasing others rather than pleasing God. Instead of working to bring glory to God, we hope to bring glory to ourselves.

Others of us hide behind our busyness as an excuse to avoid other less-interesting tasks. Meetings can seem more fun than helping your 5th grader with his math homework. Serving on the committee might bring more rewards than a night at home with your family. We crave glamorous appointments or externally affirming opportunities.

If you would rather work yourself into a state of exhaustion than seriously take inventory of your busyness, ask yourself why. What do you really want at those moments when you extend your "to do" list by yet another item or activity?

Moms Are Just Busy

For parents, fear of man can take root in many ordinary circumstances of life and quickly make the family too busy. The options for your children to participate in sports and activities begin in preschool, and they intensify each year. The pressure is on to help our kids excel. Parents no longer merely enroll their kids in sports and cheer happily from the sidelines but seek out special camps and trainers as well.

Sports, music lessons, and language classes are certainly not inherently wrong. God may see fit to make many of these pursuits part of your family, and we should teach our kids to strive for excellence. Some children have been blessed with tremendous natural abilities that their parents have the time and financial means to help them develop. But we must count the cost.

What should our ultimate goals be for our kids? We say we want them to be spiritually mature. We say we want them to grow into happy and healthy adults who love God and their families. Do our practical priorities reflect these goals?

- Do our lives revolve around worship and service to the Lord, or are our emotional and financial resources being strained to the breaking point by all the extras in our kids' lives?

- Do we tell our children that God and family come first only to continually see family time and church services neglected week after week for the sake of athletic events and enrichment activities?

- Do we tell our children that the world does not revolve around them when the ordering of our time and money indicates that it really does?

- Do we do what we do because we believe are pursuing God's best for them, or are we afraid others will think we are bad parents if we don't do those things?

- If our children excel at something, do we teach them humble reverence for the Creator that enables them to do that, or do we just enjoy basking in the glow of our children's accolades?

Fear of man can fill our days with good tasks that we accept for the wrong reasons. Mothers must especially guard their hearts and families against the fast-paced rhythms of this world. Discern what God has for your family, and teach your children through example what it means to rest, obey, and honor God with all of your commitments.

Busyness and Unbelief

Sometimes our busyness displays our unbelief in God's ability to work through others. People all around us need help and we believe it's up to us to meet their needs. We think that if we don't agree to do something, it won't get done. If it does get done, we worry that it won't be done in the manner we think best. We refuse to let some task fall short of our standard. Or we worry that future opportunities won't come if we don't seize everything before us now. Even when prayer and wise counsel indicate the timing is not right, we forge ahead.

God may choose to work through us to bring him glory and fulfill his purposes on this earth. But we often forget who is really on the throne. God is not sitting helplessly in the wings, hoping we'll come through and help him out (Acts 17:25). He can accomplish his purposes through whomever he pleases – even someone other than us! Nor is he incapable of controlling the timing. The plans he has for our lives will come to pass, on his schedule (Philippians 2:13).

A Story of Little Faith

When I first started freelance writing, a company that produced scientific materials offered to hire me for a project. I was eager to establish myself, so I jumped in without thought—or prayer.

Looking back, I'm amazed at how quickly I tamped down my first doubts. I didn't know the subject well, and the background material they sent scared me even more. Still I soldiered on, despite the big doubts that assailed me. I feared I had accepted the project hastily, feared I couldn't hack the material, feared my dreams of spending more time with my children and writing from home were futile.

What a dreadful summer! The project required hours of research, and I sacrificed a lot of time with my young children to work on it. I stayed home from fun family outings, let them watch extra television, and toiled far into the nights. After a couple of months, I realized I could not continue the pace. Humiliated, I withdrew from the project.

I made an error common to many of us when taking on a new obligation: I mistook personal desire and opportunity for divine calling: "Surely I wouldn't have this chance if God didn't want me to take it."

I thought I was exercising great faith by agreeing to this project. After all, I planned on giving God all the glory if he gave me the strength to complete the difficult job. But my faith was actually quite small. So much about the project was not right, and prayer and wise counsel made me increasingly uneasy, but I feared that this was the only chance I would get to use my gifts. What if I let this opportunity go and God could not produce another one?

My personal pride was a factor as well. I had told many people about this great opportunity. Even the hard work and difficult subject sounded glamorous. But if I quit, I would have to admit my failure, and maybe the people who hired me would be angry. There was nothing obviously wrong with accepting this project, but a thousand little things in my heart revealed I had said Yes for all the wrong reasons.

Why Do You Do What You Do?

God is not glorified in the amount of things we get done, the number of spaces we fill on our calendars, or the length of our to-do lists. God is pleased when we serve him with sincere hearts. In 1 Corinthians 3, Paul compares our works to a house that will be tested with fire. Walls built with wood, hay, or straw will burn up; only portions built with gold, silver, or precious stones will survive. In other words, when it comes to serving the Lord, quality rather than quantity counts the most.

We build with precious stones when we seek God and his glory. Gold, silver, and precious stones require us to dig deep because we only acquire them by great effort, not through quick, thoughtless gathering as for wood and straw. Matthew 6:1 states that God will not reward us for the things we do only to be seen by others. So we can see that we build with wood and straw when we busy ourselves only to please others or receive praise. Living to please others, and over-busying ourselves in the process, is idolatry.

The Bad, the Good, and the Ultimate

As Christ's representatives to the world, we shouldn't neglect our outside reputations. It's not always wrong to be pleased when others praise us. Jesus offered encouraging words to people during his time on earth, and he will again when we meet him in eternity. But praise from others is just a good thing, not an ultimate thing. Scripture clearly warns that the world will often reject us as it rejected Christ. We should serve unbelievers whenever we can: such love reveals the gospel! But we must understand that when we serve others to bring honor to ourselves, we undermine the gospel.

The Bible does promise reward for our good works, so when our motivation for those good works is just to please others, we function as if God's blessing and honor are actually unimportant. Although we may claim that God's good opinion is the only one that matters, our actions say that we believe otherwise.

On the other hand, an ordered life—a life ordered according to God's will for our lives and our families—brings glory to God. We must practice such an ordered life and teach our children how to do the same. We must help them set God's glory as their priority, too. This may require some difficult choices, but I can think of no better lesson a young person can learn than distinguishing between good things and ultimate things.

In this life, we'll never be completely free of the impulse to please others. We certainly shouldn't stop serving or giving our best simply to ensure that we won't please others! But through prayer, confession, and the work of the Holy Spirit, we can begin to put to death our sinful impulse to seek our own glory. This is possible through the grace of God.

Being Busy with the Stuff of God

Every woman has been blessed with different abilities and talents. The acts of service you do will vary according to your God-given abilities, your energy level, your family size, and your season of life. Sometimes, God-ordained circumstances will limit the amount of activities you can participate in. Other times you may be able to take on a lot of extra tasks.

This does not mean that our acts of service will always be easy. The apostle Paul, who clearly knew that God had chosen him to take the gospel to the world, speaks often of being tired and discouraged. Serving God in the activities and ministries to which he has called you does not mean that you should never be inconvenienced. As a member of the body of Christ, you will sometimes find yourself called to aid a brother or sister in great need, and meeting that need may come at a personal cost. But we must prayerfully examine the motives behind what we do, and strive to serve God with a sincere heart.

In Ephesians 6:6, we see the opposite of a people-pleaser is someone who serves God with a sincere heart. God is not glorified if we exhaust ourselves in the hope that others will praise our actions; he is most glorified when we take the attitude of a servant, like Jesus did when he washed the disciples' feet. This may mean public jobs or ministries, or quietly serving behind the scenes. We must acknowledge that God has graciously given us whatever talents, abilities, and energies we have (1 Corinthians 4:7). Then we can serve out of reverence for our Savior. Only when we humble ourselves with that knowledge can we truly serve God in a way that brings him glory.

Explore

1. Women who are overly busy must make sacrifices to get everything done. Think about the sacrifices you have made as you have chosen certain tasks and avoided or refused others:

- What have you sacrificed to do what you do?
- Have you ever agreed to do something even when you knew you didn't have time for it? Why? Did you agree to it because of fear of man, or something else?
- What does your daily calendar indicate about your priorities?
- Have you ever taken on a new project in order to avoid a less pleasant but more important task? How did that reveal your priorities and affect the rest of your obligations?

2. Apart from living for and giving glory to God, what is your main purpose in life? Do your activities reflect that?

Four
POSSESSIONS

The first piece of furniture I purchased for our first house was a couch. It was tan and cream, large and comfortable, and I loved it. When we relocated three years later, the family room in our new house was down four stairs with a sharp turn through a small doorway. We pushed and shoved and measured and twisted, but the couch would not fit.

We finally put it upstairs, where it dwarfed the tiny living room. And there it stayed for the next few years, until another relocation seemed imminent. After four years, two toddlers, and a dog, the tan and cream couch was now brown and brown. I did not want that couch to greet potential buyers when they walked into our home, but I could not get rid of the comfortable and well-built couch. My husband wanted it gone, but I argued that if we moved to a house with a larger family room, it would look lovely recovered in denim.

We bought a new couch and moved the old

couch (with more of our junk) to a rented storage unit shortly before our third child was born. Except for the monthly reminder when we paid the rent on the unit, we forgot the couch. Only when it became clear that we would not move after all would I let my husband convince me to give it away. I called a local charity to meet me at the storage unit to pick it up.

The time in storage had not been kind to my already battered couch. The storage unit remained dry but not airtight. I hadn't thought to cover the couch before storing it, and it had gotten even dirtier. The men from the charity took one look at it and shook their heads. No one would take such a sorry-looking couch. The only place it would fit well at that point was the dumpster.

We emptied the storage unit. Except for a few boxes of records, papers, and books, most of it went in the trash. And when I totaled the rent we had paid, I was embarrassed to realize that it exceeded the original cost of the couch. I had clung to that material thing because of the hope I had for its future useful-ness, and in the process, I destroyed its present and future usefulness. I loved owning that couch more than I loved using it; I loved owning it even when I didn't actually need it.

The Idol of Stuff

The love of things has become newsworthy in our

culture: stories of hoarders litter the television and Internet. We stare agog at homes where people are building walls of clothing, papers, and garbage. Cameras record these people agonizing over discarding simple things like old newspapers and broken clothes hangers. Their compulsive hoarding destroys their relationships and endangers their health. Most of them acknowledge that this behavior is irrational and destructive, but they find it difficult to change their habits.

While some of these stories may seem extreme, many of us practice similar habits on a smaller scale in our own homes. Our closets are bursting with clothes we don't wear. Our cars sit deteriorating in our driveways while decades' worth of junk sits in our garages. Rental storage units dot every neighborhood, bearing further witness to our love affair with stuff and our inability to part with it.

But It's Just a Couch

God has blessed many of us with an abundance of possessions. Yet if we are not careful, these good things can rule us. That's how I knew that my couch had become more than just a couch and signaled idolatry: I was unwilling to give it up because I thought I needed it, so my possessing it began to possess me.

How do we know when we have crossed the

bridge from "enough" to "too much"? How do you know when your things begin to rule you? Think about how you engage with things you want, the things you own, and the things you give up or throw away. Our relationship with our stuff has three phases:

- Acquisition: we obtain things
- Ownership: we use or store the things we have obtained
- Relinquishment: we get rid of the things we owned

Each phase can have healthy or unhealthy manifestations. The definition of "healthy" is when we exhibit biblical stewardship over the things we have or don't have. But when any one of these phases gets out of balance, we end up in essentially the same place as every hoarder: with too much stuff. The problem can reveal itself at any phase—at acquisition, ownership, or relinquishment—but the heart issue is the same. When we want more than we need, our possessions have become an idol.

Seeing the Idol for What It Does

The extra cost of my holding on to my first couch was easy to calculate in financial terms, but the practical and spiritual implications of having excess possessions can be harder to sort out.

What It Does to the Home

Practically, a cluttered home is impossible to rest in and difficult to clean. Simple tasks like dusting, vacuuming, and mopping become complicated by extra clutter. Stacks of random papers and fliers make necessary paperwork difficult to find. Useful items lost in a sea of junk get replaced. If we do need a stored item, it's not unusual to discover that it has become damaged during storage.

You may tell yourself that your cluttered, possession-filled home is "just the way it must be." Nothing in the Bible says clutter is evil, right? But think about how clutter has affected your family or your ability to show hospitality to others (see 1 Peter 4:9). Think about how disorganization has affected your checking account as late fees accumulate for unpaid bills lost in piles. Think about how the inability to rest in your home has affected your emotional responses to your family and others. A cluttered home doesn't necessarily mean your family is in crisis, and some circumstances could cause more harm than piles of paper and over-crammed closets. But excess possessions will rob you of your peace, add unnecessary stress to your life, and hinder your ministry to others.

It's easier now than ever to shop and acquire things. When it comes to acquisition, the 21st century has introduced temptations to idolatry far beyond anything we knew before. Just twenty years ago, we were limited to the stores geographically near us or to the catalogs available through the mail. Now, home shopping channels and the Internet give us constant access to new items. The amount of money we have earned doesn't limit us either, as credit card companies are all too happy to step in and enable us to shop more.

Excessive purchasing is not a problem limited to women, of course, but we must acknowledge the problem nevertheless. Whether due to the purchase of craft supplies, home décor, jewelry, books, clothes, or shoes, many women not only add to household clutter, but also devastate their finances through consumer debt. Even if your financial situation is not dire, many of you are stretching your finances to the limit and being poor stewards of the blessings God has given you.

What It Does to the Heart

While the practical implications of an idolatrous relationship to possessions may be more outwardly obvious, the spiritual implications are ultimately more damaging.

Idolatry in Acquisition. Consider what's ruling your heart when you acquire stuff. Why do you shop?

- You may know that your purchase is unnecessary, or even unwise, but you do it anyway, pushing aside possible feelings of guilt. Why? You just want it!
- If you want approval from others, you may attempt to secure that admiration by expensively decorating your home or always wearing the latest fashions.
- Maybe you shop to feed a hobby that consumes an inordinate amount of your time.
- Perhaps you're a bargain shopper, and you continually scour the stores for fear that you might miss a great deal if you don't.

All of these indicate that you wish to find peace and security outside of your relationship with God. You want created things, and you expect that they will provide more immediate or even lasting satisfaction than your Creator can.

Idolatry in Ownership. In Luke 12, Jesus tells a parable of a man who had more crops than he could store. The man decided to build bigger barns, and he congratulated himself on having ample provision for many years. But at the end of the parable, the man dies, and all his possessions become worthless to him. This man's acquisition was idolatry, pure and simple.

But some places in Scripture appear to paint a different picture. Proverbs 31 famously celebrates the excellent woman for her preparedness: she acquires warm clothes for her family before cold weather comes. She also manages her household well by looking ahead to her family's future needs, doing necessary work early to ensure that those needs are met. The rest of the book of Proverbs conveys warnings to look ahead, use our resources wisely, and prepare for lean times.

So what should we do? Give everything away and wait for God to come through, or hold onto everything we have in case we may need it later? The answer is . . . neither. Becoming hyper-spiritual and neglecting proper stewardship does not solve the idolatry of possessions. But hyper-controlling your stuff and failing to rely on God does not solve the problem of horrible stewardship.

Look back at the parable of the man with the barns. Jesus follows this with instructions not to worry about our lives. This context reveals that the grain-storer's problem is not necessarily that he stored his excess grain, but that *he believed that by doing so he had ensured a secure future*. Since the first barns had apparently been adequate in any normal circumstances, the fact that he had to build bigger barns implies that he kept more than he really needed. Like the woman in Proverbs, he looked ahead to the coming winter and wanted to prepare for it, but she made reasonable preparations whereas he tried to stave off worry. He reassured himself with words spoken straight out of his heart: "[Y]ou have ample goods laid up for many years; relax, eat, drink, be merry" (Luke 12:19).

Idolatry in Relinquishment. Clinging to excess possessions indicates a fundamental distrust in God and his provision. Rather than use our abundance to bless people in need, we cling to our possessions and our money because we believe that we have the obligation and power to prevent poverty and want.

I have stored useless items—from cook pots with broken handles to stained clothing—out of fear that "I might need it someday." How much better to discard those things immediately to make room for what I really needed, or simply to de-clutter and make our home a more pleasant place for friends and family? How sad that I hung onto a closet full of unworn clothing when so many could have been blessed with those items. That reveals functional unbelief: as though the God who created the universe can save my soul but not really provide what I need for daily life. Should I find myself in a situation where only a cooking pot with a broken handle would do, he is able to meet that need!

We proclaim that we trust God to meet our needs, but the boxes of junk in our basements and garages tell a different story. We may honestly confess that we know our clutter represents what we *want*, not what we need. And we may justify our clutter as wise preparedness. It's okay—even biblical—to buy things ahead of time, to store food for future use, to have savings accounts and retirement plans. But when we look to those things for security, foolishly imagining that we have the power to prevent bad things from happening, they become idols.

Ruled by Wisdom Or Fear?

Do you see a pattern here? Everything in this book comes down to the motivations of your heart.

- Do you bargain shop to be a good steward of your resources and have more to give, or are you fearful of the future and futilely trying to obtain peace through possessions?
- Do you store items that you know you will need in the foreseeable future, or are you paralyzed from getting rid of things by a sea of what-ifs and unlikely scenarios?
- Can you afford the clothes and shoes you buy, or do you live beyond your means, hoping to impress others with the things you have?

The determining factor is fear. If fear motivates your acquisition, ownership, or relinquishment, you are not trusting God. Snagging that designer handbag or clinging to unused possessions "just in case" or to get the praise of others may bring a temporary feeling of security, but like all other idols, the comfort never lasts.

Remember that God Is Sovereign

Life tends to go in cycles. As it says in Ecclesiastes 3, we have a season for every purpose. Preparing for coming needs, whether by buying items ahead or saving money, is a wise use of resources. But if we begin to think that we have the power to prevent calamity by clinging to material things, we behave as foolishly as the rich fool in Luke 12.

We read many stories of people who faced tragedy in the Bible, but the common denominator in all of them is that God remains on his throne. Jeremiah and Habakkuk mourn devastation caused by their nation's sin. The book of Job chronicles the life of a man who suffered through no fault of his own. But none of this happens outside of God's attention, care, and rule. We may not ever understand why bad things come into our lives, but the Scriptures assure us that nothing happens outside of God's sovereign control.

God never promises a life free from trouble, but he does promise to always be with us and walk with us through our storms. Plan for the future and ration your resources wisely, but remember that God's grace alone allows us to get through this life. Serve God and others with open hands and an open heart, trusting in the sovereign God who holds the future.

Explore

1. When it comes to handling your possessions, do you struggle more with acquisition, ownership, or relinquishment? Think of an example for each piece of the path of stuff in your life.
2. Have you ever held on to something you didn't want or need because it was too nice just to give away? Have you ever felt guilty about getting rid of something you owned? Is this good stewardship? Why or why not?
3. The old adage says you should not have anything in your home unless you find it useful or beautiful. Is that true of you? How so, or how not?
4. Has your life been negatively affected by excess shopping or possessions? What would your husband say? What about your friends? Your children?
5. Consider a fast from purchasing. How hard would it be for you to not buy a new (or new to you) piece of clothing or item for your house for a year, a month, a week, or a day? Why would that be hard for you?

6. How has your life been negatively affected by excess shopping or possessions?

Five
LEISURE

In my third year of college, I was assigned a ten-page term paper for a class. I loved the class, but dreaded the paper. This was in the days before the internet, when research had to be collected the old-fashioned way: real paper, real pens, real books ever reminding me of the writing awaiting me. The pile of note cards, journal articles, and library books seemed to mock me every time I passed my desk, because I was putting off the real work of writing.

The professor kindly granted me an extension, yet I still put off the paper until the very last moment: he wanted it in his office when he arrived Monday morning. To ensure that it was waiting for him then, I needed to turn it in before the academic building was locked at ten o'clock Sunday night. I rearranged my work schedule so that I could go to church that morning and then grind away at the paper all afternoon and evening. It would be close, but I thought I could get it done.

Then something else came up. A tall, handsome, soft-spoken young man new to the church asked if I would be there for the evening service. Hoping there might be more to his question, I rushed home and dashed off the paper, shoving little more than a typed rough draft under my professor's office door on my way to church. My hunch was right: the man invited me to dinner.

I have no idea how I did on that paper. That professor did not return term papers, and I was far too embarrassed about the paper's poor quality to ask for feedback. But the relationship begun that day seemed like a good tradeoff for the lousy grade: I married the man from church 14 months later.

Of course, most procrastination stories do not end so happily. I worked far harder on that Sunday afternoon than if I had worked steadily over the semester, and the product was terrible, but I did finish on time. What if something serious had come up that day and kept me from the paper that afternoon? An illness, perhaps, or some emergency? That was my last chance, and I had no other draft to fall back on. The stress I caused myself by simply looking at the pile of research day after day and not doing anything about it seems foolish in retrospect. Every weekend, I told myself I would rest first and work on the paper later. But that was not real rest; it was an excuse for self-indulgence.

Real Rest, Real Work

Perhaps it sounds too harsh to now call my desire
for rest a kind of selfishness. After all, rest is good,
right? The practice of setting aside a day for rest and
worship has long been regarded as good for Christians both mentally and spiritually. We were made
for work (Genesis 1:28), but God never intended
for our work to define us. But I was going beyond
taking good and necessary rest. What I really wanted
was time to myself to do what I wanted to do

We live in a society that works hard but views
work primarily as a means to an end. By "work" here,
I mean many different occupations – jobs that may
take us outside of our homes and jobs that may not,
including the different tasks that suit different stages
of life (married, mothering, single). We generally do
our work simply because we think we have no other
choice, and in the back of our minds, we often wish
for another way. We long to win some sweepstakes
so we can live a life of ease, hiring out every bother-
some and mundane chore. Even more, we long for
weekends, vacations, and at long last, retirement – the
day when we will never have to work again.

As appealing as that dream may be, it's not
biblical. When God created Adam and Eve, he gave
them work to do (Genesis 1:28), and while they
were in the Garden, they enjoyed their work. After
the fall, sin and the chaos it brings entered God's

perfect creation, tainting every good thing about life – especially our relationship with God, but also our relationships with others, and our work. At one time, these brought nothing but joy, but now they bring sweat, angst, hurt, and fear.

Nevertheless, no honest reading of Scripture permits us to forsake walking with God or developing relationships with others just because they are hard. We are now destined to toil by the "sweat of our face" (Genesis 3:19), but work is still a gift from God, given to us for our good. Indeed, Solomon tells us there is nothing better for us than to find enjoyment in our work, which is from God (Ecclesiastes 2:24-25). Paul specifically instructs the older women in Titus 2 to teach the younger women to be busy at home. We have much good work to do!

When "I'll Do That Later" Becomes Your Way of Life

Some learn their lessons early, but the chaos of procrastination has long been a way of life for me. I remember, in grade school, collecting leaves in the dark for a fall foliage poster, and in college finishing my lab reports in the car as my roommate drove us to class. After I became a mother, the first cold Sunday of the fall often found me frantically searching through storage boxes for suitably warm children's clothing. So much for Proverbs 31:21!

I had plenty of warning for all those events. The due dates for each assignment were given far in advance. And though I've never known the exact date for the first cold snap, it comes to this area at roughly the same time each fall. For many years, I thought I was just forgetful or aloof and that the last-minute frenzy was forgettable and harmless. After all, I still had food to eat, so I must not have been quite so bad as the sluggard in Proverbs 24:30-34, right?

The connection between laziness and poverty may not seem quite as clear in our culture as it did in the agricultural world of the Proverbs: resting while you should be working brings poverty because the crops don't get planted and harvested, which means there is no food to eat. This puts a new spin on 2 Thessalonians 3:10, where Paul says that anyone in the church unwilling to work should not eat.

Procrastination costs us in modern life as well. Waiting until the last minute to do an assignment steals my joy and robs me of creative time to do the project correctly, often requiring others to wait on their own related work until my piece is finished. Our families exist on expensive drive-through meals because we do not take the time to shop for groceries and prepare meals at home. Our homes require costly repairs because we fail to prioritize routine maintenance. We pay unnecessary late fees rather than send the bills on time. We run late and upset to appointments because they weren't scheduled in conversation with the rest of the family.

In this kind of life, all of our relationships suffer – especially our relationship with God. When everyday life is a race from one urgent deadline to the next, we withdraw from open fellowship with God and submission to his will. We narrow into a world in which we call all the shots. We retreat into a small realm that we feel we can control, believing the lie that we control our own lives.

We've lost sight of how submitting *now* to the work God has for us *now* is good. Instead, we justify procrastination as merely *postponed* work, and we excuse laziness as a common and therefore accept- able vice. We regard procrastination and laziness like junk drawers in the kitchen: universal and necessary. Everybody needs "me" time, so we don't try to hide our lazy excuses or feel ashamed of our procrastina- tion. It's all just the way things are.

Are we then obligated to live in this chaos? Are we doomed to do our work late, with haste, begrudg- ingly, or stressfully? Are some people always going to be procrastinators? No, a habit of procrastination indicates a worship problem: an unwillingness to do the work that God has appointed for us, or an inability to discern what he has given us and what he has not. The procrastinator loves to hoard her time for herself rather than work diligently in it on the errands and tasks God gives her. She would rather blame the chaos outside of her than the chaos in her heart.

For the Truly Overwhelmed

Some of you may be cringing and sighing as you read this chapter, because you do desperately need some downtime. The next chapter is designed especially for women with difficult circumstances, so I encourage you to read on. Yes, many women are up before dawn and busy with hardly a break until well after dark. You rarely have time to relax, and you don't want to feel guilty for the few times that you do. Your life may be out of balance in other ways, but not because you are overindulging in rest and leisure.

We need to consider ourselves carefully here. For some of you, that will be true and I run the risk of discouraging you unnecessarily. Let me humbly suggest, however, that many women are in the midst of an entertainment glut. Just like eating too much of a rich chocolate dessert can make you sick to your stomach and ruin an otherwise delightful meal, over-indulgence in leisure can cast a pall over every aspect of your life.

Perhaps you need to prayerfully reorder your life in order to work and rest well. Many of us have taken an unbiblical view of work, no matter how much work we actually do, and that perspective affects every aspect of our lives in unhealthy ways. Some of us may be working too much while some of us have entirely too much leisure time in our lives. Indeed, many of us are addicted to leisure activities that take priority over what God has actually given us to do, and we need to be honest about the reasons why.

Addicted to Leisure

In the book *Women Helping Women*, edited by Elyse Fitzpatrick and Carol Cornish, Penny J. Orr lays out some of the symptoms of addiction. We tend to think of addictions as problems with alcohol, drugs, or gambling, but many other things can function as addictive activities in our lives. Many women are addicted to TV, social networking sites, shopping, reading, and other hobbies.

While none of these activities are necessarily evil in and of themselves, if you indulge in them to the extent that they prevent you from doing what God has ordained for you to do, they are sin. You must first prayerfully discern what God has called you to do, and then you can discern whether you are using leisure to postpone needlessly the work ordained for you. How do you know when you have crossed the line from engaging in a proper hobby to idolatrous pursuit of leisure? How do you know when your hobbies, or leisure in general, have become addictions or idols in your life?

You are dishonest about the time you are spending on an activity. If you are reluctant to admit to others how much time you spend on a hobby, that's a sure signal that something is wrong. You might wait for the rest of your household to go to bed so you can watch TV or play on the computer without witnesses. You might find yourself telling a friend that you stopped by the mall for a "few minutes" to shop when it was really closer to two hours. You may use your fussy toddler as an excuse for not having time to shop for groceries when you spent a good portion of the day reading a novel while the child played.

Are you a wise steward of your time? Do you prayerfully schedule your days for what God has called you to, including appropriate time for real rest?

Your hobbies or activities negatively affect your finances. Women who overindulge in shopping often have high credit card bills to show for it. Or perhaps you have bought so much clothing that you can no longer store it in your home (see the chapter on possessions). Knitters and quilters joke about their "stashes," and readers maintain that one can never have too many books, but if you spend more money on these activities than your family can afford, it's no joking matter. Similarly, the time spent with these hobbies may mean that you end up spending extra money on restaurant meals and convenience foods. If your hobbies cause you to spend more money than you can afford, or if you hide bills and purchases from your husband, you need to prayerfully examine your priorities and habits.

Do you submit your hobbies to a budget suited to your family?

You rely on electronic babysitters. Children require our time and attention. If you're a stay-at-home mom, it's tempting to tell yourself that your children get plenty of your time simply because you are with them during the day. Many of us have good intentions on limiting the time our children spend with electronic media like television and video games, but we can easily put those good intentions aside when we want to spend extra time doing our own thing.

Physical presence may not mean mental or emotional presence: are you present to your children?

You bristle at suggestions that your life is out of balance. A woman who overindulges in a leisure activity, even one that is not inherently bad, can become defensive if she feels her hobby is being threatened. If even gentle, loving suggestions that you need to reduce the amount of time you spend on an activity make you feel angry, perhaps it's time to examine yourself. That kind of response can indicate a worship problem: you want that hobby more than you want a calendar that honors God.

How do you respond when confronted with advice you don't want to hear?

Leisure as Idolatry

At the beginning of the book, I defined idolatry as relying on anything other than God for peace and happiness. If we apply this definition to lives out of balance due to an overindulgence in leisure, we see that for many women, leisure functions as an idol.

Each of us has been placed where we are by a sovereign God (Acts 17:26). We have been given husbands and children to care for (Titus 2), employers to serve (Colossians 3:22-23), and other good works to do to build up the body of Christ. But all of these tasks are important, and all of them bring glory to God. Even the most mundane of household tasks is an act of worship if done humbly to the glory of God.

When we ignore the tasks we know we should do (which means that we understand that these tasks are assigned to us by God), we are essentially saying that our comfort and pleasure are more important than the needs of our families. When we do our chores sloppily and halfheartedly, we operate on the belief that God doesn't really know what is best for us. When we eschew our chores for our own hobbies, we show that God does not seem trustworthy to give us the rest we need, so we must take it for ourselves. Since idolatry is relying on created things to give us what only God the Creator can give, leisure is an idol for many women.

We may use leisure to try to escape or block out thoughts of the mundane or overwhelming tasks in our lives, but we are usually not successful in this. Like a staticky radio playing in the background, your unfinished chores may nag at you, sucking joy and real rest from your life. Meanwhile, great blessing awaits us. There is no greater joy than humbly and obediently submitting to God's will for our lives. Romans 7 says we are constantly at war with our sinful nature. For many, rallying to get up and work when we really want to rest or play requires an enormous leap of faith. But God promises to give us everything we need to perform the task at hand.

Finding the Balance

I hope this chapter has provided you with a fresh way to consider leisure. But if you've always known that you lack motivation, you may feel I've kicked you when you were already down. So here is a hand to help you get up: a few practical steps you can take.

Schedule Time for Rest and Leisure

No one would argue with the idea that you need regular meals, but the idea that you need to schedule real rest and appropriate leisure may seem ignoble. It's tempting to go from one extreme to the other, either indulging excessively in hobbies or cutting them entirely from your calendar, but we need to find a reasonable, middle ground. If you are accustomed to doing without sleep in order to indulge in your favorite hobby, you need to get yourself on a regular sleep schedule. Exercise is also an important practice that many women ignore. Your body is a temple of the Holy Spirit and you need to steward your health well.

One of my favorite things to do is read. When I was a kid, I often got in trouble for reading too much and playing too little, but during college, I seldom read for pleasure. I felt guilty reading for enjoyment when I had pages of assigned class reading to do. Unfortunately, that guilt didn't cause me to diligently apply myself to my studies; I still wasted a lot of time. Instead of spending leisure time on reading, I wasted it on activities I didn't enjoy nearly as much: I frittered away valuable hours in front of the television or wandering around the dorm. In reality, I needed the distractions and breaks, but I felt guilty resting, so I attempted to assuage my guilt by convincing myself that these were accidental distractions.

Ironically, it would have been much more efficient to plan on times to play and then thoroughly enjoy those times as a restful and delightful gifts from God.

Make Your Schedule a Matter of Prayer

We rightly ask God to guide our finances as we aim to be good stewards of our money, but we rarely ask that he guide our calendars and help us want to be good stewards of our time. Lay your tasks before the Lord. Prayerfully ask him to guide you in your days. Then get up to work, trusting that he will sustain you and give you the rest that you need.

You may see others doing ministry activities and hobbies that you also desire to do, but step into them prayerfully rather than just sincerely. Study the Scriptures to understand God's will for you: You may be surprised to find clear responsibilities for your station and season of life. If you have a hobby that you particularly enjoy, you may be reluctant to schedule time for it even if you determine that you have the liberty to pursue it, afraid that you will be unable to exercise self-control once you get started. Ask a trusted friend to pray for you and your schedule. Ask her also to hold you accountable and to ask you the hard questions about your desires and your activities, about your work and your rest.

Live Your Life in Seasons

Some seasons of life are more demanding than others. A mother of infant twins will not have the same control over her schedule as a woman with an empty nest. The mother of busy teenagers no longer must help her children dress and eat, but she may spend many afternoons shuttling her kids to activities and practices, or stay up many late nights talking over the latest adolescent crises. Regardless of the particular difficulties brought by your current season of life, you will probably look back on it with some measure of fondness. Don't spend time regretting the past or wishing for the future. Remember that this is where God has you right now, and ask for the grace to find joy in your tasks.

Trust God to Give You the Rest and Pleasure You Need

In Psalm 139, David praises God for his sovereignty and foreknowledge of our days. God knows our words before we speak them, and he knows each day before it occurs. Nothing that happens to you is outside of God's sight. He promises to be with us at all times, and he promises that no temptation will come to us for which he will not provide a way to escape and endure (1 Corinthians 10:13-14). God knows the work you must do, and he knows the amount of time and energy you have. You can trust him with your work, your rest, and your leisure. You can trust him to heal your chaotic, procrastinating heart.

Explore

1. Think back to a time you were overwhelmed. What helped you complete the difficult task or the large number of tasks before you? If you did not complete your task(s), what prevented you from doing so?
2. We usually procrastinate because that makes us feel like we are in control. How does procrastination actually make your life more hectic?
3. Do you rest after you complete your work or before? How has excess leisure cost you?
4. How can you tell when a favorite hobby or activity has become idolatrous? Where do you struggle with this?

Six
DIFFICULT CIRCUMSTANCES

In writing this book, one of my main concerns has been that it would leave women feeling more hopeless than helped. Some of you are going through seasons of great strain and suffering. The idea that the chaos in your life is stemming from your own sin might send you spiraling further into despair.

As I stated earlier, not all feelings of guilt are unwarranted. Jeremiah 17:9 reminds us that we are not honest with ourselves when it comes to sin. It is woven into our fallen human nature to try to convince ourselves that biblical admonitions don't apply to us or our current situations.

But the dynamic can also work in the other direction. Sometimes, due to a sensitive spirit, people are unduly convicted when they really need to be clinging to God's grace. I am reminded of this in my work with teenagers. On occasion when I have reminded them to pay attention during teaching time, I have received heartfelt apologies from my most respectful students, while the ones to whom the reminders were directed seem to remain unfazed.

Two particular groups of women have been on my heart as I wrote this book: single mothers and women with health problems. I'm also sure there are other difficult situations that I cannot even dream of. While I hope some of the advice in this book has been helpful to you, I am also mindful that your burdens are heavier than some. While you still have a responsibility to be obedient to God and his commands, I would like to offer you some additional words to help you keep things in perspective.

God Knows Your Situation

You may be feeling very lonely right now. Trials often leave us feeling isolated. It may seem that no one notices your situation, let alone offers sympathy and help. If you're single, you may feel like your church is composed entirely of happy nuclear families. If you're suffering from an extended illness, you may feel that people have moved on with their lives, forgetting about you and insensitive to your struggles.

You may even feel that God has forgotten you. This is not unusual. In Psalm 13, David feels abandoned by God and cries out:

How long, O Lord? Will you forget me forever?
How long will you hide your face from me?
How long must I take counsel in my soul
And have sorrow in my heart all the day?
How long shall my enemy be exalted over me?

It's common to feel that God has deserted you: common but untrue. Everything that has happened to you has happened under the watchful eye of our sovereign God. He knows all the days he has ordained for you (Psalm 139:16), and everything that happens to you is part of his plan (Acts 17:26, Ephesians 1:11).

This includes every detail of your life. He knows the times you feel burdened and overwhelmed. He knows when your desire to work is hindered by weakness and pain. He knows the length of your to-do list and the limits of your time, energy, and strength.

And even though it may feel that he's not there and not listening, the Bible reminds us that those feelings are untrue. At the end of Psalm 13, David reminds himself of what he knows to be true:

But I have trusted in your steadfast love;
My heart shall rejoice in your salvation.
I will sing to the Lord,
Because he has dealt bountifully with me.

He Means It for Your Ultimate Good

God also promises that for those of us that follow him, everything that happens to us happens for our good (Romans 8:28). This is hard to say, and I'm sure it's even harder to hear. But the Bible is firm on this point.

It's important to remember that our idea of what is good for us is often different than God's. The verse that follows Romans 8:28 reminds us of this: "For those whom he foreknew he also predestined to be conformed to the image of his Son, in order that he might be the firstborn among many brothers."

God's idea of our good is not always an easier and more comfortable life. Our highest good is to become "conformed to the image of his Son," or to become more like Christ. That is what "good" *means*. Sometimes God does this by showing us mercy that causes our hearts to swell with praise. At other times, he allows suffering to enter our lives. We might not be able to see the good behind our suffering, but we can trust the Bible when it tells us that God is always good.

The Old Testament Books of Job and Habakkuk both contain the heart-cries of men going through hard times. While neither man receives a detailed explanation as to why God works in the manner he does, both men realize that God is sovereign and worthy of praise in all circumstances. I love the closing verses in Habakkuk 3:17-19:

> Though the fig tree should not blossom,
> nor fruit be on the vines,
> the produce of the olive fail
> and the fields yield no food,
> the flock be cut off from the fold
> and there be no herd in the stalls,
> yet I will rejoice in the LORD;
> I will take joy in the God of my salvation.
> God, the Lord, is my strength;
> he makes my feet like the deer's;
> he makes me tread on my high places.

We should all strive for the kind of faith that can say these words in times of trial.

Difficulties Are Not an Indicator of Your Unworthiness

The Bible teaches us that every good gift comes from the hand of God (James 1:17) and that we should always praise God and give thanks. It's important to develop a heart of thanksgiving, and it's important to give praise to God for the good things that happen in our day-to-day lives.

Many Christians have taken this to heart, giving

God the glory when car keys are located, parking places are convenient, good sale prices are found, and medical tests are negative. This is well and good; I have given thanks to God in every one of these situations.

But what about the times when the keys remain lost, the parking places are far from the entrance, the prices are too high, and the medical results are positive? Does that mean you have fallen outside of God's favor? Does he love you less? Are your prayers less effective than the prayers of those whose lives are going smoothly?

It's easy to fall into this faulty thinking. The important thing to remember is that God's ways are different than ours (Isaiah 55:9). In the book of Job, we learned that Job was allowed to suffer because God knew he would remain faithful. In the story of the man born blind in John 9, Jesus tells his disciples that the man's blindness was not the result of sin, but so "that the works of God might be displayed in him."

Even if your difficulties can be directly tied to sin, your circumstances are still within God's sovereign care. This does not absolve the sinner from responsibility. Sin should still be repented of, and forgiveness can only be obtained through Christ's work on the cross. But you can rest in the knowledge that sinful actions of your own or of others have not derailed God's plan for your life.

Perhaps your health problems are tied to bad

decisions and irresponsible actions in your past. Perhaps you find yourself divorced through no fault of your own. You can still move forward and glorify the God who is always there, regardless of the circumstances.

These are difficult truths, and I have only scratched the surface. The coexistence of God's sovereignty and our personal responsibility is difficult to understand. It's certainly beyond the scope of this book and my skill to explain it adequately! But we do know that the Bible teaches both divine sovereignty and human responsibility. We should be repentant about sinful actions in our lives. We should praise God when he graciously allows seasons of happiness, but we should also praise him when life is hard. God uses all the circumstances in our lives to conform us to the image of Christ. Whether that comes through difficulty or ease, we should remember that becoming more like Christ is the most blessed thing that can happen to us, and praise God however he chooses to bring that about.

It may seem strange that I spent so much time talking about the sovereignty of God in a book on organization. I just wanted to remind you that God does not plunge us willy-nilly into difficult circumstances. When we believe that our lives are only workable if God manages things in the manner we prefer, anxiety and fear will rule our hearts. It is only when we truly accept that God is sovereign over our present circumstances that we can fully trust him for the solution.

In other words, hopelessness and despair are rooted in unbelief about God's power and goodness. When we trust that God is in control, we can have the "perfect peace" spoken of in Isaiah 26:3. Pages of practical suggestions will be of little help if your heart is flailing about in despair. By first reminding yourself to trust God, you can then move forward, knowing that he is in control.

That being said, there are practical things you can do, even in seasons when you feel especially burdened. Many of these are ideas I touched on in earlier chapters. If your current load is heavier, the situations surrounding them are probably more complex as well. I hope that by bringing them out separately, I can make it easier for you to apply them to your life.

Prioritize

This is something that all Christians need to learn to do, but nobody more so than woman carrying a particularly heavy burden. You cannot do everything you want to do, no matter how selfless or worthy a task it may be.

If you are a single mother with children at home, your primary ministry is your family. Since you are the only parent in the home, you also need time to recharge your own emotional batteries. This is going to limit the amount of time you can commit to outside activities, including outside ministries. Rather than continually serving in children's ministries, you may need to take some time to go to an adult class or session to be fed yourself.

Women with health concerns also need to guard their time and energy carefully. Giving the bulk of your time and energy to your family is not short-changing the Lord. You can serve him by serving your family.

This is hard to do. So many worthy ministries need so much help, it's difficult to say no when the need is great. Also remember that ministry leaders are human as well. Even if you say no with great grace and sincere regret, you may come away feeling misunderstood or that you have let someone down. Just remember that God is in control. You are to strive to please the Lord, not other people.

But just because your time is limited doesn't mean you get a free pass from serving. First Peter 4:10 says that we have to be good stewards of God's grace and serve one another according to our gifts.

You may not be able to arrange and direct the Christmas cantata, sew the costumes, and paint the scenery, but there are other things you can do to serve. If you have children, prayerfully seek ways you can serve that involve them as well.

You can also commit to being a prayer warrior. My church puts out a weekly prayer list. The needs on that list are often overwhelming. It's so encouraging when people in the church faithfully pray over those needs. Some of the people whose ministering has had the most impact on me have been those who have faithfully prayed for me and encouraged me with kind words, calls, and cards.

Practice Contentment

In the Christian classic, *The Rare Jewel of Christian Contentment*, Jeremiah Burroughs describes Christian contentment as "that sweet, inward, quiet, gracious frame of spirit, which freely submits to and delights in God's wise and fatherly disposal in every condition."

This does not mean that you never try to improve your situation, nor does it mean you have to be pleased about sad circumstances in your life. It also doesn't mean that you can't share with others about things that are troubling you. What this does mean, though, is resting in the Lord, knowing that he is in control of all things in your life. You may not be able to see the reasons behind the problems in your life, but God knows them all. You can trust that everything that is happening to you is to make you more like Christ, and you can rest in that.

One of the quickest routes to discontentment

and discouragement is to compare your situation with that of others. It's easy to think of how different things would be if you had the time/energy/money of other women you know. This is especially different if these women seem lazy or unappreciative of what they have. Just remember that God called you to glorify him in all circumstances, including the ones you are in right now.

Ask for Help

The Christian life was never meant to be lived in isolation. The New Testament instructs us to be part of local churches, to submit to our church leaders, and to serve our brothers and sisters in Christ. You may be in a season where you need to be a recipient of the church's help, from either the church as a whole or individual members.

The early church took the duty to care for those in need very seriously. The people in the church shared their material possessions with each other. Special attention was given to the care of widows without families or financial resources. In 2 Corinthians 8, Paul speaks of how the Macedonian church gave beyond its means to help the church in Jerusalem.

Some churches have special procedures in place to assist those in need. Whether it is designated money to meet material needs or groups of volunteers who are skilled to offer practical help, there are countless creative ways to get help to the people who need it. Other churches may not have formal committees, but they may be full of loving people who are ready and willing to lend a hand to someone who needs it.

But the most prepared committee or dedicated church member will not be able to help if you don't make your needs known. It's not sinful to admit that you need help. While many Christians have experienced times when God met their needs before they even made them known, the biblical model is people telling their brothers and sisters in Christ what they need, so that those brothers and sisters can then help.

You may have serious needs that you haven't shared with anyone. You may be feeling that you should keep those needs between yourself and God, so you are waiting for him to miraculously supply them. Nothing is beyond God's ability, but please prayerfully examine your motives. It's often humbling to admit that we need help. Don't let pride stop you from seeking the help you need.

Life is full of difficulties. The amount of suffering in the world is one of the hardest things for us to understand. Attempts to offer comfort often fall short and wind up sounding like empty platitudes.

Rather than closing this chapter with yet one more platitude, I'll give you God's answer to the apostle Paul. Paul was given a "thorn in the flesh," the details of which we are not told. The Lord chose not to remove this trial from Paul's life, but gave him this promise in 2 Corinthians 12:9: "My grace is sufficient for you, for my power is made perfect in weakness."

His grace is sufficient for you as well.

Explore

1. Have you ever been in a situation where you needed extra help from the body of Christ? What kind acts from others did you find most helpful?
2. What are practical ways you can minister to a woman in need?
3. If you are currently in difficult circumstances, how can you still serve in your local church? Identify your spiritual gifts and pray about opportunities to use them in your church. Ask others to pray with you about this.

Seven
WHERE TO BEGIN

For a while now, I've thought that organization is a lot like weight loss. Most of us already know what we need to do, we just have trouble doing it. I don't need to read a book on how to lose weight. I just need to eat right and exercise. For me, right now, I need to stay out of the chocolate cake sitting in my kitchen and go out for that run I've been putting off by working on this chapter. My hope for this book has been to help you see the stumbling blocks that keep you from doing the things you know you should.

But it's not that clear for everyone. Just as most of us know at least one naturally thin person who finds calorie-counting a foreign concept, some of you might feel helpless to identify the steps necessary in becoming organized.

The idea of cleaning a house or keeping a calendar might be so overwhelming for you that you don't know where to start. Perhaps you come from an environment where disorder ruled. Or maybe you grew up in a home where household chores where hired out. If you recently left the working world to stay home, the open-ended, continuous cycle of housecleaning might have you reeling.

When my oldest two children were preschool age, I worked outside the home full time while my husband finished his degree. During that time we were blessed to have a hired housekeeper come in weekly to handle the heavy cleaning. Although I was grateful to return home when our third child was born, I was sad to see our weekly housecleaner go. It was on one of those first days home that I went upstairs to clean the bathroom.

The sound of running bathwater brought my two oldest up to investigate. With confused faces, they asked what I was doing. I was amused to realize that for as far back as they could remember, most of the housework had occurred while they were out of the house. I explained to them that I was cleaning the bathtub; they had no idea such things needed to be done.

I promised at the beginning of the book that this was not going to be a "how-to" on cleaning and organization, but if the basics of housekeeping seem scary and mysterious, they are not hard to learn.

Information Is Not the Issue

The house I grew up in had "kitchen carpet," so I didn't pick up a mop until I had an apartment of my own. Through trial and error, and following the directions on the back of the kitchen floor cleaner, I have come up with my own method for cleaning my floors. With the internet, it's even easier to find this information. When I typed "how to mop a floor" into a search engine, I got over 4 million results. "Cleaning a bathtub," the chore that so amazed my children, got 3.8 million results.

If you aren't sure how often things are "supposed" to be done, you can search "house cleaning schedule" or "house cleaning checklist" for guidelines.

If you prefer books to the computer, head to the library. Most books on home organization will be under the call number 648. Don't be shy about asking the librarian for help. You won't be the first person to ask for books on housekeeping, and you won't be the last.

Just be warned that these are to be used as tools, not as some kind of alternate Bible. These books will offer you the method of one person which worked for their personality type and a particular set of circumstances. Yours may be different. Glean from their wisdom, but don't feel bound to follow their exact schedule or approach.

Find a Schedule That Suits Your Personality

As you develop a schedule, try to think about what works best for you. Most schedules divide the larger household chores over several days. (This is the wisdom our grandmothers used as well: Monday is wash day, Tuesday is ironing day, etc.) I personally vacuum on Monday and clean the bathrooms on Tuesday. Some people dislike this type of schedule, though, and would rather do all the heavy cleaning on one marathon day.

I have a friend who saves all her laundry for Thursday. She dislikes doing laundry, and finds doing a little bit of laundry every day too depressing. Although I haven't ever tried it myself, the thought of saving all my laundry for one long day makes me feel like my head might explode. But it works for her, and both of us manage to keep our families presentable, so I can't say that either of us is wrong.

Time Yourself

Take note of how long some of your more frequent tasks take. If you have a general idea how long it takes you to do something, it's easier to make a realistic plan, and harder to justify putting it off. I have a dislike of folding laundry that borders on the irrational, so I tend to put it off if I can find anything else to do. Imagine how surprised I was to find that

I can have a load of laundry folded and put away in just over ten minutes. Upon learning that, it's much easier to get it done, especially since I know that my baskets of clean clothes will build up to an hour-long folding session if I don't get them taken care of.

Having a realistic idea of the time required for daily tasks will also help you if you tend to over-schedule yourself. I've tried many times to cook supper, work on memory verses with the kids, mop the floor, and make a snack to share in the hour between soccer practice and Wednesday night small group, but I just can't do it and arrive at church on time in a godly frame of mind.

Find a Calendar You'll Use Regularly

The choices for calendars and organizers that are available are endless, but the most detailed calendar in the world won't work if you don't record activities in it and check it regularly. As much as huge wall calendar, color-coded for each family member appeals to me, it will hang, virtually untouched, on my wall. I learn about most appointments when I'm away from home, so a small calendar that I can fit in my purse is my best bet. I have a nifty calendar on my cell phone, but since I can write things on a pocket calendar more quickly, I'm staying old-school for now. If you need a central place where all family members can check and record their schedules, a large wall calendar may be what you need. You may also like a computerized or web-based calendar that your entire family can access.

Beware of the List

Every how-to book on home organization seems to bring in a checklist at some point. It appears that people who are naturally organized love to make lists and check them twice. My computer-programmer husband thinks that most of the world's problems can be solved with the right flow chart. My mother finds crossing things off her to-do list so satisfying that if she completes a task that's not on her list, she writes it down just so she can cross it off.

I tried for years to make detailed lists, just as my husband and mother do. I've finally given up. I have a basic idea of what days the big chores need to be done, and I may write down a few things that I don't want to forget in the course of the day, but I've abandoned the idea of a detailed list.

This isn't to say that lists are bad, they just need to be realistic. I sabotaged myself by starting my daily lists with:

1) Clean out all closets
2) Clean out all drawers
3) Clean garage
4) Eat lunch

If you find a list helpful, however, by all means, use one. Just remember that it is a tool. An unrealistic list will be more of a hindrance than a help. If you struggle with excess leisure, a long, detailed list will be tempting to ignore altogether. Women who struggle with busyness and perfectionism may try to work themselves frantic trying to get to everything, and feel like they've failed if things remain undone.

Plan Ahead

Most of the decisions and actions that plunge us into the traps of busyness, perfectionism, leisure, or possessions are made quickly. We happen upon a great price on shoes and decide to buy. A new opportunity presents itself and we commit on the spur of the moment. We go over to dust the bookshelves and decide to alphabetize and rearrange. The day looks bleak and gloomy so we ignore the housework and curl up in front of the TV.

Once you've identified areas in which you are weak, make a plan for dealing with them. What is a realistic budget for your family? How much room do you really have for shoes and clothes? How many extra commitments can you reasonably handle? How much time can you devote to hobbies and leisure to keep a healthy balance?

Even though it ultimately boils down to self-control, having a plan will help you think on your feet. If you've exceeded your clothing budget for the month, there's no need to troll the mall looking for sales. If you have decided to limit yourself to a set number of ministry opportunities, you will have to eliminate one of them before you take on a new project. If you can look forward to relaxing when your paperwork is done, you're less likely to fritter away time set aside for bill paying by playing Free Cell or dithering on Facebook.

Commit to Lasting Changes

Sanctification is a process. The habits that cause chaos in your life are deeply rooted. You probably won't conquer them instantly. If you find yourself sliding back into old habits, it doesn't mean that change is impossible. Christ frees us from the penalty of our sin, but the roots of sin will remain in our hearts, needing to be battled, for as long as we live. But though the presence of sin will linger, you can never exhaust the mercy and grace of God. Every day brings a brand new opportunity to start afresh and bask in his love.

When we leave bad habits behind, we often have to deal with the repercussions of previous choices. Excessive shopping can lead to debt and financial problems. Clinging to excess possessions leaves behind piles of clutter to deal with. Long bouts of pro-crastination can cause general disorder in your home or finances. It may be tempting to look at the work ahead and decide that change is just too much work. You think it would be simpler to continue as you were.

If I may return to the dieting analogy, successful dieters are those who commit to a longterm lifestyle change. A crash diet may get you into that bridesmaid's dress, but the weight loss won't be lasting.

Christ's death and resurrection ensures that all our sins are forgiven, but the earthly consequences of sin usually remain. A lifetime's worth of clutter will not be eliminated in an afternoon. Years of bad financial management won't be sorted out in an hour. Commit to change, and prayerfully seek the Lord's strength as you do so, but be prepared for discouraging days. Conquering sin takes time and effort, but the peace that you have afterwards is always worth it.

Seek Help if You Need It

God never meant for us to go it alone. One of the functions of the church is to walk alongside each other in seasons of struggle and sorrow. Acknowledging your sin and repenting is always the first step in sanctification, but if your problems are severe, you might need extra help.

All of us need the salvation that only Christ can offer, even if your life is organized and peaceful. But severe problems with organization can leave big consequences in their wake. Don't be afraid to seek out a biblical counselor for help. If the chaos in your life has devastated your finances, a Christian financial counselor may be needed. It may be humiliating to admit how far you have strayed, but bringing your sin to the light of day and receiving the loving assistance of a fellow Christian will help God's sweet grace and mercy to blow through your life and bring healing to your heart.

Closing Thoughts

It's a hard task writing a book like this. I have been reminded time and time again of my weaknesses and how I constantly fall short. The writing of this book coincided with one of the busiest periods of my adult life, and at times it felt comical that I was writing a book on organization. But God is faithful, and while I am always aware of my weaknesses, I am also blown away that a holy God loves me and is using the daily happenings in my ordinary life to make me more like Christ.

__Seasons and callings.__ The last thing I want to do is create unnecessary guilt by imposing arbitrary standards. We have all been called to different tasks; we are all at different seasons of life. An extro-verted, high-energy woman with no children at home might thrive on a schedule that includes lots of outside commitments, while a woman with a demanding job or many young children may need to scale things back. Your family might require an orderly, organized home. It may need to always be clean so that you can relax if last-minute guests come. Another family might require less order, but plenty of freedom to create and play.

That's why housecleaning schedules, charts, and spreadsheets often don't work. It's difficult to place your own life—with its particular struggles, concerns, and callings—atop a grid someone else has created.

Face your sin. The problems I have highlighted in this book are not usually the type of things that we think of as sinful. They certainly don't cause the same degree of devastation as sins like adultery or stealing. But it is the little foxes that spoil the vineyards (Song of Solomon 2:15). Your struggle with one or more of the problems highlighted in this book doesn't mean you are headed down the road to destruction, but any of them can hinder your relationship with God, which is something we must always try to overcome.

I have noticed two extremes among Christians when it comes to dealing with these so-called "little sins." One is to make a joke of it. We probably all have too much stuff, too many commitments, or spend too much time goofing off. Instead of repenting and trying to change, we make a joke of it. We reassure ourselves and others that since we all have these problems, it's really not that bad.

The other extreme is to hide our shortcomings. We paste on a smile and pretend that we don't have issues like this. Others may have these kinds of struggles, but we certainly don't.

Neither attitude is healthy or holy. James 5:16 instructs us to confess our sins and shortcomings. But with that confession comes the responsibility to try to change, to allow the Holy Spirit to work in our lives to make us more like Christ.

As I said in earlier chapters, we must put aside these idols that we have placed on the thrones of our hearts. This is not an overnight fix. We developed these patterns of behavior because they gave us comfort; it's hard to let these things go, even when we know better. But by identifying sin patterns in our lives, by examining the true motives in our hearts, we can finally begin to release our grip on these idols and finally relinquish them to the Savior.

Know your calling. The real challenge is to determine what God has called *you* to do. If you're married, it also means determining what kind of lifestyle best serves your husband. Submission has been an unpopular topic since Genesis 3, but part of our calling as wives is to adapt our lives to best serve our husbands and families.

You also need to identify any heart issues that may be hindering you in your calling. Have you taken on too many commitments? Are you putting off important tasks while you fill your days with worthless pursuits? Are you filling your house with unneeded possessions and clutter? Are you setting unrealistic standards for yourself and others around you? Understanding the reasons you do these things is a helpful step in conquering these sins.

Persevere by grace, for the glory of God. It is the Holy Spirit that stirs in us the desire to be holy. But becoming more like Christ requires effort on our part as well (Philippians 2:12-13). We don't do this to attempt to make ourselves worthy of God's love (which we can't do, anyway), but to bring glory to God and enjoy a fuller relationship with him.

The link between God's grace working through us and our personal effort in becoming more Christ-like is hard for our human minds to comprehend. But we do know that the Bible teaches both. And if you've been walking with Christ for any length of time, you've probably learned that although putting sin to death requires great effort, the rewards of peace and joy that await us always outweigh the initial pain.

The task of sanctification never ends. Until we arrive in glory, there will always be more work to do. It is my prayer that this little book will assist you in this struggle by helping you identify unhealthy motivations in your life, and urging you along on the path to holiness.

Sources Cited

- Sultan, Aisha. "Welcome to 1956: 'Time capsule' house on the Hill is perfectly preserved" March 7, 2009. http://www.stltoday.com/lifestyles/article_71a08b6a-eb50-50ff-932f-f32b1f4a8f9e.html
- Priolo, Lou. *Pleasing People* (P&R Publishing, 2007)
- Fitzpatrick, Elyse and Cornish, Carol. *Women Helping Women* (Harvest House, 1997)
- Burroughs, Jeremiah. *The Rare Jewel of Christian Contentment* (Banner of Truth, 1964)

ABOUT CRUCIFORM PRESS

What would a book-publishing company for gospel-centered Christians look like if it began with the realities of 21st century technology?

We think It would focus on Content, Simplicity, Reliability, Trust, Convenience, Voice, and Community. Here's what we mean by that. These are our promises to you.

Content: Every book will be helpful, inspiring, biblical, and gospel-focused.

Simplicity: Every book will be short, clear, well-written, well-edited, and accessible.

Reliability: A new book will be released the first day of each month. Every book will be the same price. Each book will have a unique cover, yet all our books will maintain a distinctive, recognizable look.

Trust: If you like this book, then you're probably a lot like us in how you think, what you believe, and how you see the world. That means you can trust us to give you only the good stuff.

Convenience: Our books will be available in print, in a variety of ebook formats, and frequently as audiobooks. Print or ebook subscription opportunities can save you time and money.

Voice: We want to know what you'd like to read about, or who you think we ought to consider as an author, or really anything constructive you'd care to say about what we're doing and how we're doing it.

Community: We want to encourage and facilitate the sense of community that naturally exists among Christians who love the gospel of grace.

JOIN US. Sign up for our newsletter at **CruciformPress.com**

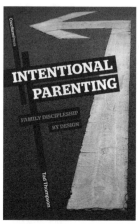

Intentional Parenting
Family Discipleship by Design

by Tad Thompson

The Big Picture and a Simple Plan — That's What You Need to Do Family Discipleship Well

This book will allow you to take all the sermons, teachings, and exhortations you have received on the topic of family discipleship, make sense of it, and put it to use.

"As parents, we know God has given us the responsibility to train our children in his ways. But many parents don't know where or how to start. Tad has done us all a favor by identifying seven key categories of biblical teaching we can utilize in teaching our children godly truth and principles. This easy-to-follow plan will help any parent put the truth of God's Word into their children's hearts."

>**Kevin Ezell, President, North American Mission Board, Southern Baptist Convention; father of six**

"Here is a practical page-turner that encourages fathers to engage the hearts of their families with truth and grace. In an age when truth is either ignored or despised, it is refreshing to see a book written for ordinary fathers who want their families to be sanctified by the truth. Thompson writes with a grace which reminds us that parenting flows from the sweet mercies of Christ.."

>**Joel Beeke, President, Puritan Reformed Theological Seminary**

"Need an introductory text to the topic of discipling children? Here is a clear, simple book on family discipleship, centered on the gospel rather than human successes or external behaviors."

>**James M. Hamilton, Associate Professor of Biblical Theology, The Southern Baptist Theological Seminary**

Our Top Seller

Wrestling with an Angel
A Story of Love, Disability
and the Lessons of Grace

by Greg Lucas

*The riveting, inspiring true story
that readers have called
"a touchstone book of my life,"
and "alternately hilarious and
heartbreaking," a book that
"turns the diamond of grace in
such a way that you see facets
you never really noticed before."*

"C.S. Lewis wrote that he paradoxically loved *The Lord of the Rings*
because it 'broke his heart' – and Greg Lucas' writing does the same
for me."
> ### Justin Taylor, Managing Editor, ESV Study Bible

"Witty... stunning... striking... humorous and heartfelt. *Wrestling with an
Angel* provides a fresh, honest look at one father's struggle to embrace
God in the midst of his son's disability. Can sheer laughter and weep-
ing gracefully coexist in a world of so much affliction? Greg knows all
about it. I highly recommend this wonderfully personal book!"
> ### Joni Eareckson Tada, Joni and Friends International

"You will laugh; you will cry. You will feel sick; you will feel inspired.
You will be repulsed by the ugliness of sin; you will be overwhelmed
by the love of God. Greg Lucas takes us on an unforgettable ride as he
extracts the most beautiful insights into grace from the most painful
experiences of life."
> ### David P. Murray, Puritan Reformed Theological Seminary

"Greg Lucas is a captivating storyteller. When he writes about life with
Jake, I recognize God's grace and loving persistence in my life. I want
more!"
> ### Noël Piper, author, and wife of pastor and author John Piper

Reclaiming Adoption

Missional Living Through the Rediscovery of Abba Father

Dan Cruver, Editor

John Piper, Scotty Smith, Richard D. Phillips, Jason Kovacs

Do you doubt God's delight in you? Understanding God's adoptive love for you as your Father will free you to live boldly in this world **from** *God's acceptance, not in order to gain it.*

"This remarkable volume will inform your mind in a wonderfully biblical way, but also convict your heart, energize your will, and inflame your affections as you contemplate what God has done in making you his child."
Sam Storms, Pastor and author

"We need the ancient wisdom of the Bible, not another glory story from some cool church. Dan has brought us near to the heart of God. As you read, you will sense the need to embrace your own acceptance as God's adopted child."
Darrin Patrick, Pastor and author

"*Reclaiming Adoption* captures the heart and soul of what it means to be a child of God. This isn't simply a book on adoption. It's about the reason we were created and how we are to spend the rest of our days loving others."
Tom Davis, Author of **Fields of the Fatherless**

"*Reclaiming Adoption* is a must read. It will tell your head who you are and move your heart to live in response."
Steve Chong, Director of the Rice movement, Sydney, Australia

Also endorsed by *Russell Moore, J.D. Greear, Ed Stetzer, Jedd Medefind, Shaun Groves, Burk Parsons, David Evans, Mike Wittmer, Tim Chester*, and many more.